CARVING THE COYOTE

Dale Power

Text written with
and photography by
Jeffrey B. Snyder

Schiffer Publishing Ltd

77 Lower Valley Road, Atglen, PA 19310

Printed in China.
ISBN: 0-88740-567-3
We are interested in hearing from authors with book
ideas on related topics.

Designed by Mark S. Balbach

Published by Schiffer Publishing Ltd.
77 Lower Valley Road
Atglen, PA 19310
Please write for a free catalog.
This book may be purchased from the publisher.
Please include $2.95 postage.
Try your bookstore first.

Contents

Introduction

I'll always remember camping as a boy and waking to the sound of a prolonged howl followed by a series of yips. I pulled the sleeping bag up tight around my neck and shivered. Didn't anyone else hear? If they did, no one spoke, leaving me to wonder if the pack of coyotes would sneak into camp after me, since I was the only one awake. Today I know better.

Able to leap fourteen feet and travel at speeds ranging from twenty-five to forty miles an hour, this grizzled gray coyote will dine on whatever presents itself, including mice, insects, fruit, snakes, rabbits and an occasional deer.

Though persecuted by people, the coyote is spreading into new terrain, East to Pennsylvania and South to Florida. As the natural predators of an area are killed off, coyotes have moved in to fill the niche. In California, they've moved to the suburbs. They've even been spotted in New York City.

As the coyote population has grown and gained our attention, they have become choice animals to carve and collect.

My coyote is carved out of Basswood, also known as American Linden, because of the forgiving nature of the wood as well as the high quality and durability of the final product. It is classified as a hardwood, but I find it great for either hand or machine carving.

While we're speaking of carving, I used a bench knife, a set of assorted hand gouges, an Optima-1 Wood Burning System, an Optima-2 high speed grinder and assorted carbide burrs for this project. The paints used are acrylic washes.

Whenever you use power tools, it's always wise to protect your lungs with a dust mask or dust collection system like the one you'll notice in the photographs.

Good luck carving your coyote.

Pattern reduced **75%.**
Enlarge **133%** for original size.

Carving the Coyote

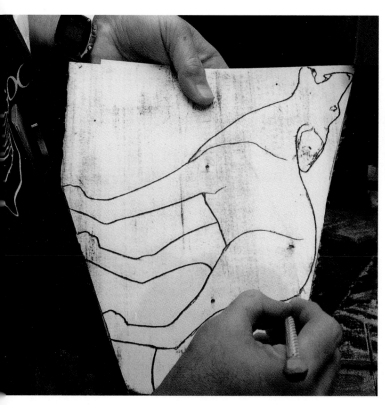

Trace the pattern on to 3/4 inch thick blocks of basswood

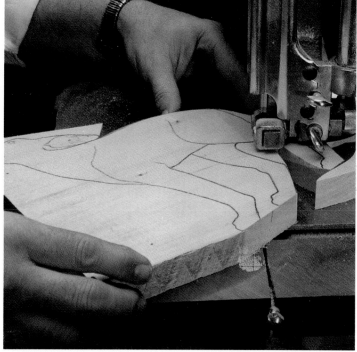

Cut the coyote out around the pattern on the block.

To follow Dale step-by-step through this book, proceed from the upper left, down the left column, then to the upper right and down the right column. It's just like reading a newspaper.

Cut out the three indicated patterns on three basswood boards, glue them together with yellow carpenter's glue and clamp them with rubber bands. Allow the glue to set for twenty-four hours to insure that the pieces will not separate.

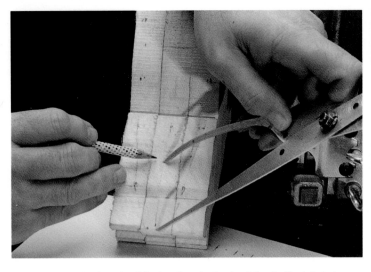

Measure the length of the head to the back of the skull, right between the ears. This head is the basic measurement for the rest of the coyote.

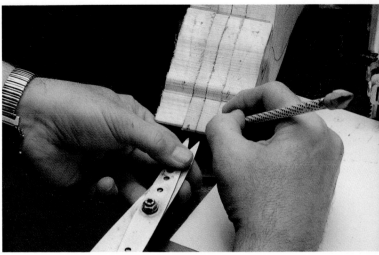

The nose measures 1/4 of the length of the head.

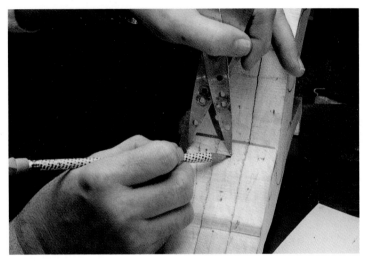

We are going to draw the dorsal (back) view of the coyote onto the basswood blank. Start by drawing the centerline. This will keep your piece balanced. Go ahead and sketch the center line clear around, it is easier to keep it balanced this way.

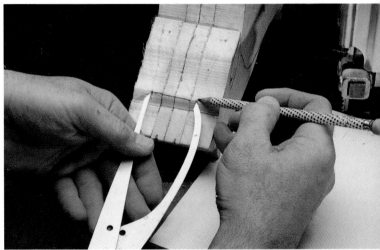

At the top of the eye orb, measure one half of the length of the head. Make sure to draw a line at 90 degrees to the center line between these two points. This makes sure that your points will be straight across from each other.

The tail is not in all three segments of the glued basswood block. It is off center, and the center line must follow it and become the center line between sections two and three.

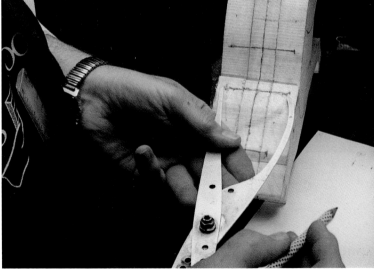

This is the broadest point of the front shoulder, it is 5/8 of the total length of the head.

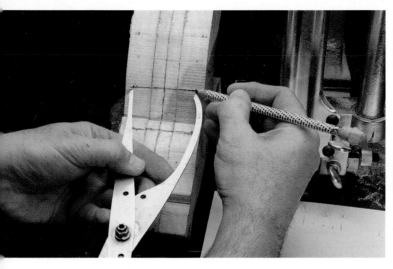

Mark the widest point of the belly next. It measures 3/4 of the length of the head from side to side.

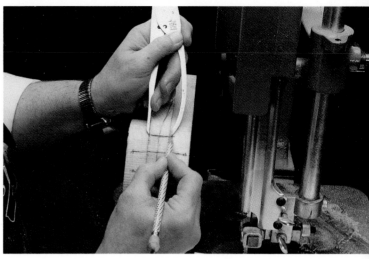

The final measurement comes at the root of the tail. The tail is 3/8 of the length of the head wide at the root. Taper the tail slightly to the tip.

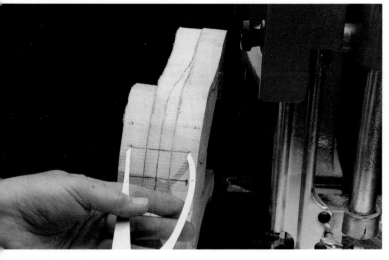

The next measurement falls just in front of the back hips, it is 3/4 of the length of the head.

Now you get to play connect the dots. After connecting the dots, run your line off at this point to allow room for the rear leg to be carved.

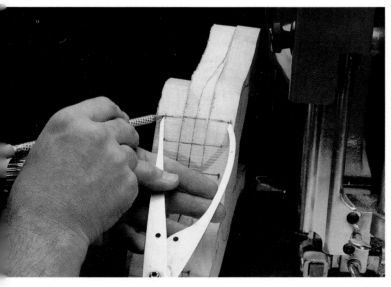

Followed by the measurement which falls at the widest point of the hips and is 7/8 of the length of the head.

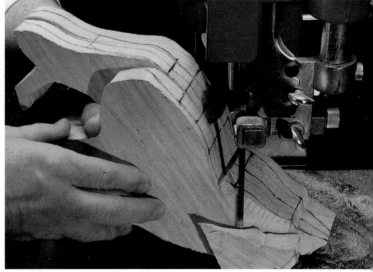

Lay the coyote so that he is braced solidly and slab off the side of the face along the dorsal guide lines.

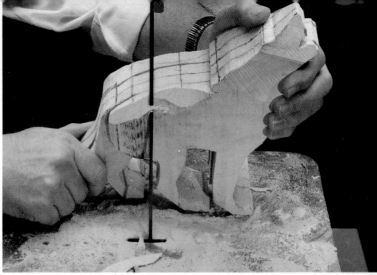

Now cut along the lines from the tail forward. Remember keep your fingers braced along the coyote's sides and not through the legs or you will cut your fingers. If your saw is not high enough you can remove the stock with a coping saw.

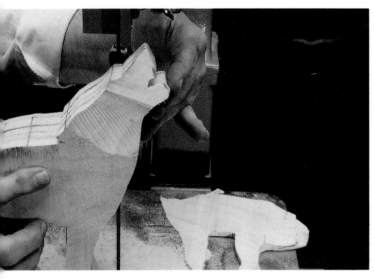

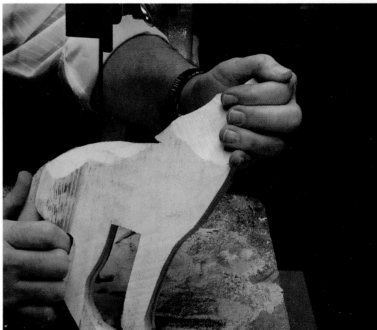

The stock has been removed from one side and the other is being cut along the dorsal guide lines.

While being very sure where your fingers are, start rounding off the sharp edges. Use very little pressure to avoid the band saw yanking the piece away from you. Take off little strips at a time.

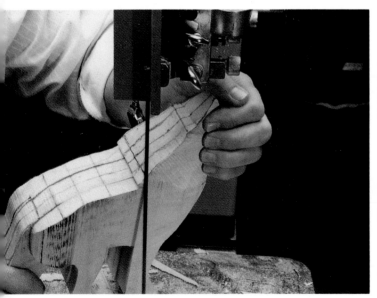

Now we will begin to remove the excess wood by rounding it off.

Do the same thing on the underside of the neck.

8

Now you can see the rounded surfaces under the neck.

Do the same thing along the back line of the flank between the hind leg and the tail.

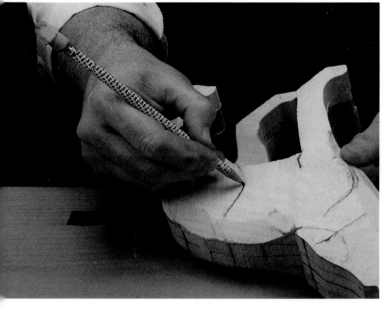

Redraw the profile of the coyote, making sure that the elbow is shown. It has to be carved up on the side of the animal, up on the body. Repeat ón both sides.

And along the back side of the elbow.

Start with a bench knife and make a stop cut along the back flank, about 1/16 of an inch deep.

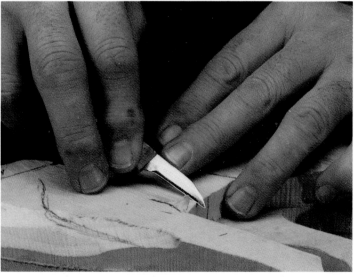

Remove some of the meat to the stop

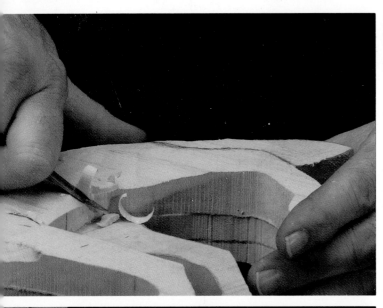

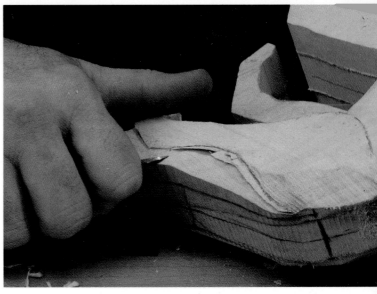

Do the same thing along the back line of the flank.

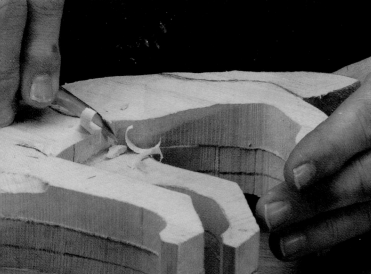

Remove material from the belly back to the stop at the hind leg. Cut down to cut away the loosened material.

Along the back of the leg deepen the stop cut to 1/8 of an inch deep along the back of the hind leg.

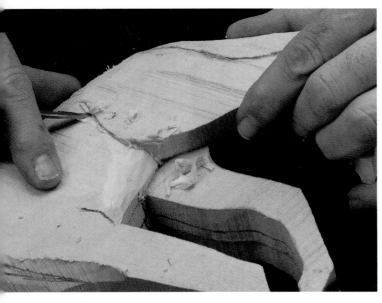

Make a little paring cut to open up the stop cut along the back flank. This gives dimension to the leg.

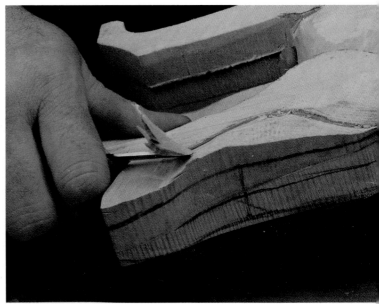

This allows you to snap off larger pieces to remove waste wood faster.

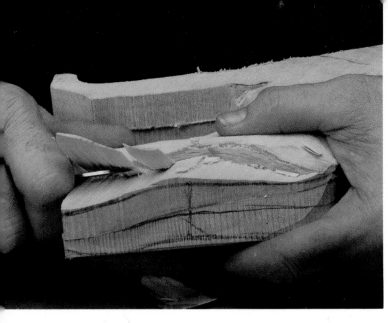

Remove waste wood down to the dorsal guidelines.

The front and back paw pads should align.

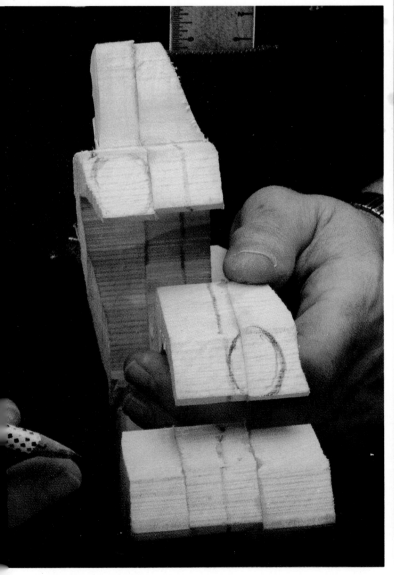

Draw circles on the bottom of the feet for the pads. Begin with the back foot because it will align directly with the front foot and will show you where to place the front pad. The circle should be roughly the size of the end of your thumb and all must be the same size.

Remove the excess wood, marked with an X in the photograph.

11

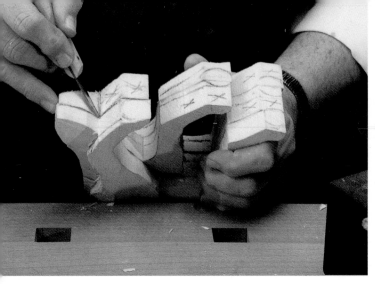

Score deeply along the side the leg and beside the tail.

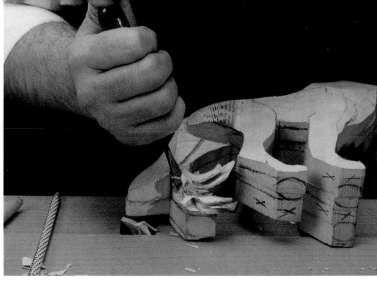

Drive straight down along the tail to remove the excess wood.

Score the line on the underside of the tail as well.

Repeat the process along the length of the tail.

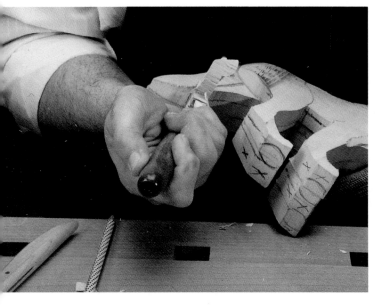

Using a square gouge, loosen the waste wood in small amounts along the underside of the tail and along the rear leg.

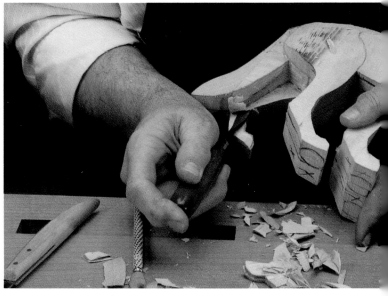

This is how it should look with the material removed along the back leg and the tail.

Make a stop cut along the forward back leg in preparation for removing the waste material along the inside of the leg. Score the line several times to make it deep enough.

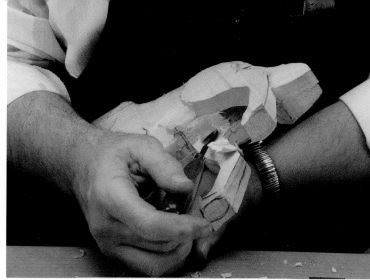

Nearly done. Do not remove the waste wood from the outside of the leg yet. It will provide support while you remove the waste from between the front legs.

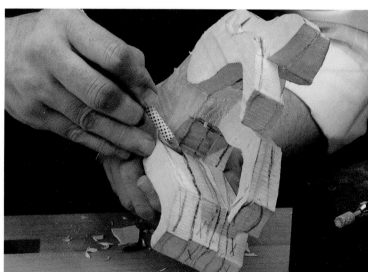

The inside line of this front leg should come to the chest just inboard of the glue line.

Slab off the excess material, making sure to support the leg with your thumb. When you get close enough to the leg, redo the stop cut.

The inside of the other front leg should come to a point the same distance from the center line as the first leg.

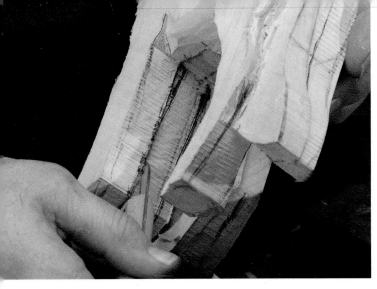

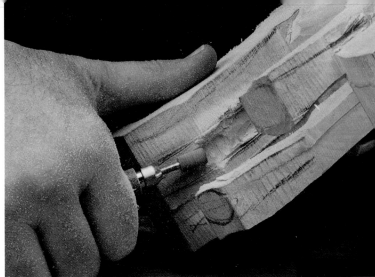

Make a stop cut along the inside line of both legs. Score to the outside of the line. It is best to cut fat, more wood may be removed but none can be added back.

Remove the waste with the Kutzall. It works well in areas that would otherwise be awkward to reach with a knife. Stroke the Kutzall like a knife.

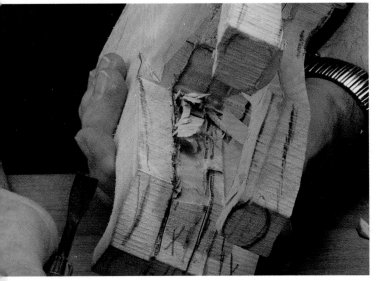

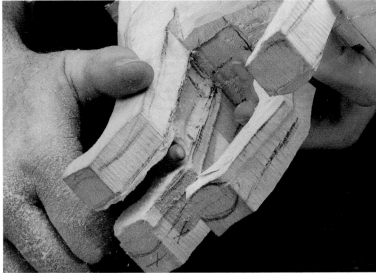

Take the square gouge and slab away the waste material between the score lines. Go down either side of the lines to open them up so you can cut to them. Push the gouge in towards the center of the coyote.

This opens up the legs without applying pressure on them.

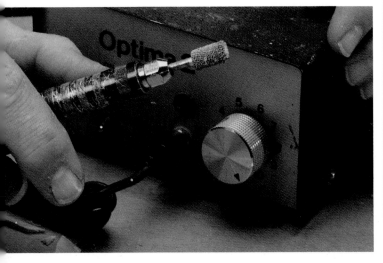

Once you have begun to open up the area between the front legs, use a high speed grinder with a drum Kutzall to remove more of the waste material.

Use the Kutzall to this point. Then switch to a round gouge to remove the material near the chest along the inside of the leg. A wood carver's safety glove is useful to prevent the gouge cutting the hand supporting the coyote. It is also important to use only the power of your wrist when cutting toward yourself.

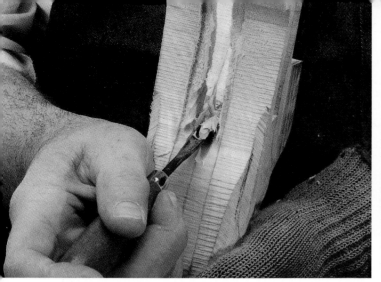

Continue to clean out between the legs.

Continue until the legs look like this.

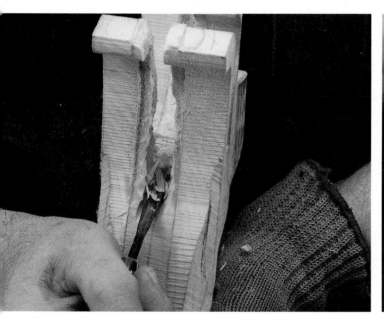

Cut from the chest back towards the belly to round that area.

Score the line along the outside of both front legs now. Don't worry too much about detailed shaping as such yet. Work on removing waste wood for now. You will finish shaping in a while.

Roughly shape the insides of the legs with the gouge and the kutzall.

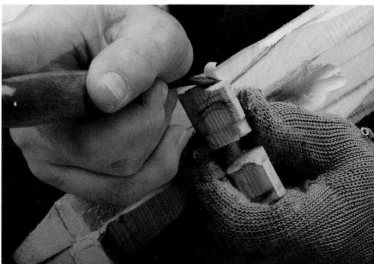

Remove the waste wood around the foot first with a square chisel. Support the foot with your thumb along the bottom side.

15

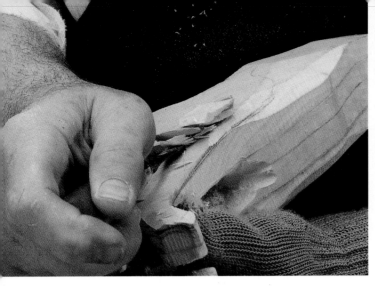

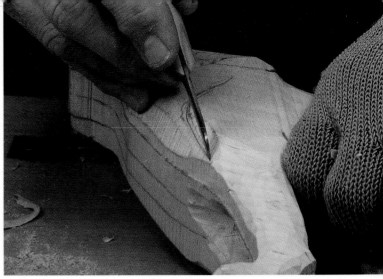

Move up the leg, removing waste wood with the gouge. Leave extra wood along the inside of the leg at the angle of the wrist for the dewclaw. Always carve from the foot up. That way you carve towards a stronger area of the leg.

Now make a stop cut along the front of the shoulder, so you can reduce the neck down to free the front leg and create the dewlap between the front legs, hanging from the chest.

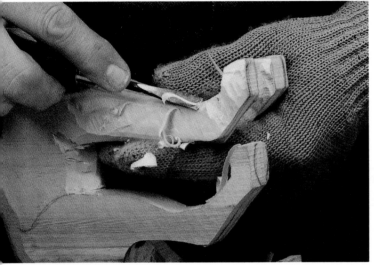

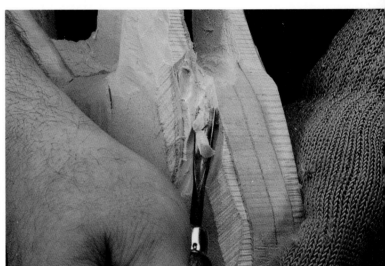

Continue to waste away wood from the leg with the square gouge. The front leg is shaped roughly like a flattened teardrop, coming to a semi-rounded point in the back. Aim for the center line along the back of the leg for the tip of the teardrop. Do not forget to support the leg with your fingers as you waste away material. It is becoming more fragile as you carve.

Shape the neck to create the dewlap with a medium sized U gouge.

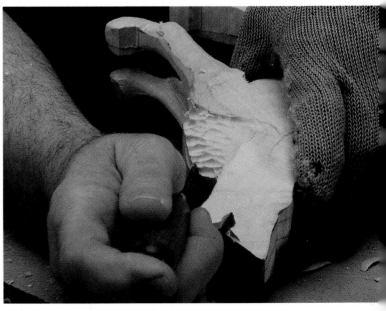

When you have finished with the gouge, the leg should look like this. Repeat the process on the other front leg.

This will also begin to create the ruff in the neck.

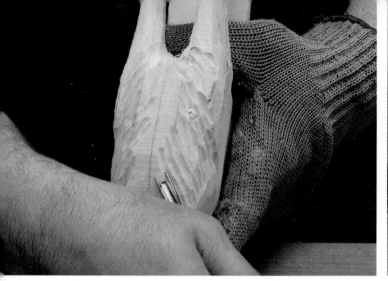

Angle in towards the center line when creating the ruff.

Trim the face down square. Remember to keep the jaw balanced. It should be the same distance from the center line on both sides.

When you are finished with this step the ruff should have this shape. Imagine water running down the coyotes neck. It would follow these angles.

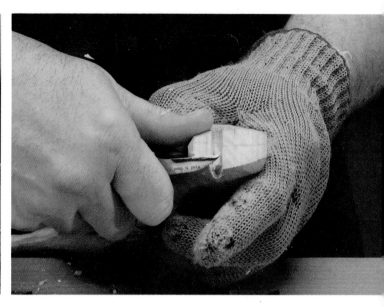

The base of the lower jaw now becomes a rounded point.

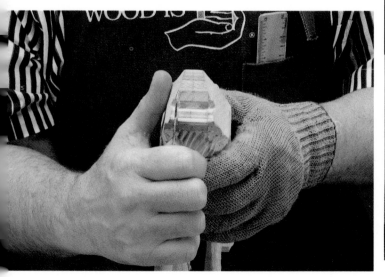

The sides of the face should be square. If they are not square after slabbing off the sides of the face, trim them down.

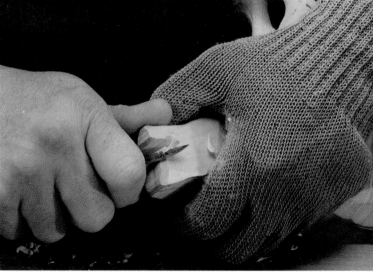

Now the edges along the upper jaw must be rounded in towards the center line. The face has to be done well. It is the most technically demanding aspect of the coyote.

The cut made to form the eye should be square, the eye should not slope out at the bottom of the cut.

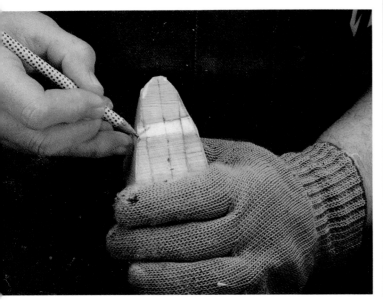

This is the angled guide line for the eye. Follow this angle closely.

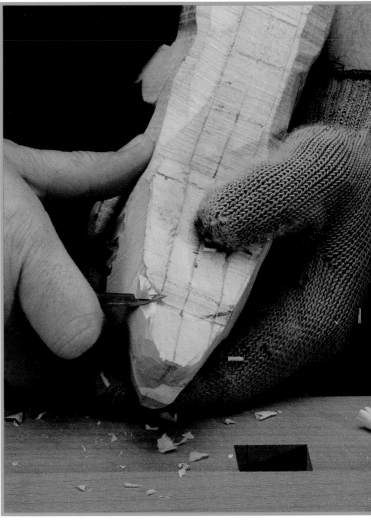

Make a cut along the bridge of the nose into the eye socket itself to finish the cut.

Use a levering cut to carve straight down to create the eye.

This is the finished square cut for the eye.

Once the eyes are cut, trim the muzzle off to round the upper edge.

Sketch in the lips as well.

Stop the trimming just in front of the eyesocket to create a ledge for the eye.

When you are done, it should look like this.

Indicate the nostrils for a cutting guide. If you have a pet dog, take a look at the nose. It is built differently than you might think.

The point of a bench knife is used to make a triangular cut to create the nostrils.

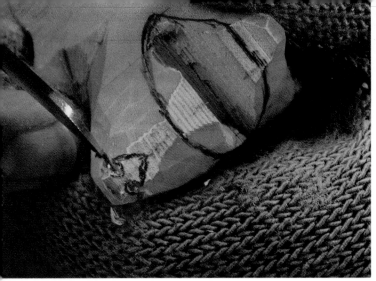

Make a stop cut out along the edge of the nostril about 1/16 of an inch deep to create the running edge of the nostril.

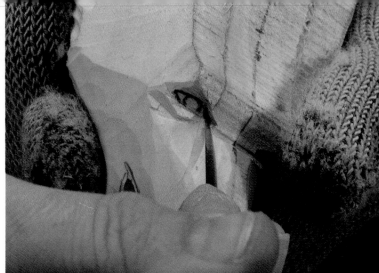

Use just the tip of your bench knife to cut first from the inside corner, or tear duct, of the eye along the line of the upper lid.

Angle up with a small cut to the stop cut to create the edge of the nostril. Be gentle or you will cut through your stop cut. You might want to restrop your knife first to make sure it is sharp. Repeat this process on the other side, making sure to keep both sides the same.

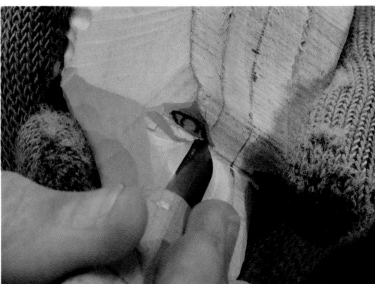

Next place a cut along the edge of the lower lid.

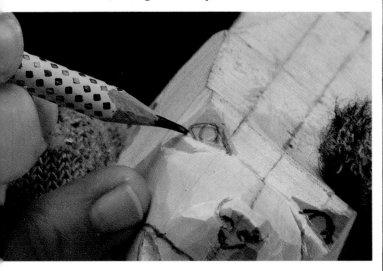

Sketch in the eyes. Make sure the pupils are an equal distance from the center line or the coyote will look cock-eyed.

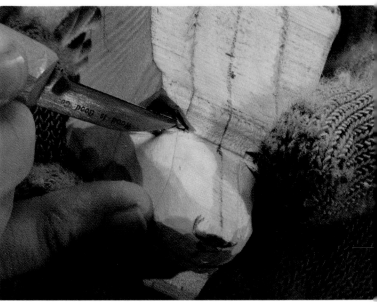

Now make a cut from the edge of the pupil towards the tear duct.

If this is done right, a triangular wedge should pop free creating the inner half of the eye, defining the inner edge of the pupil.

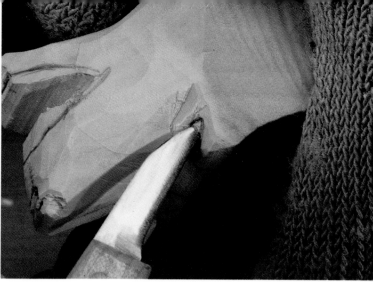

The third cut is along the eyeball pushing into the corner, poping a small wedge, defining both the eye and the pupil.

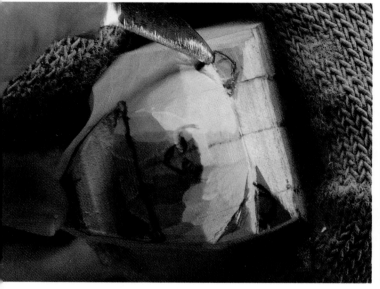

Repeat the same process along the outer edge of the eye. First cut along the bottom edge towards the eyeball.

Cut upward along the upper lid line with a series of short cuts, pressing upward to create the look of an upper lid overlapping the pupil.

Cut along the upper edge ofthe lid towards the eyeball.

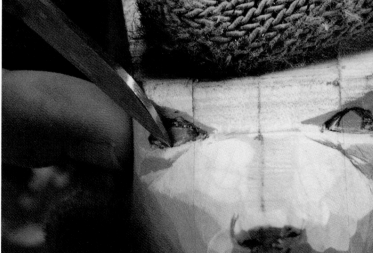

Cut downward in a series of short strokes, pressing the tip of the knife in along the lower lid to create the lower lid line and the image of the eye set down below this lid.

Define the upper lip with a stop cut 1/16 of an inch deep.

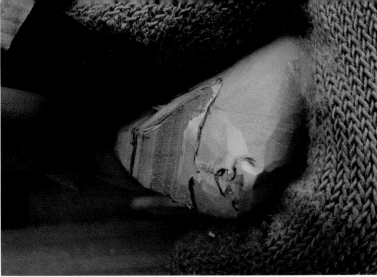

Now make a stop cut line along the lower lip, using a levering cut with your thumb to propel the knife and give you a finer cut.

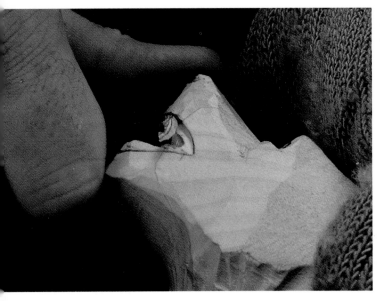

Now cut from the underside of the lip, taking off a small sliver of wood to define the edge of the lip and the upper teeth. This process will also straighten the upper teeth.

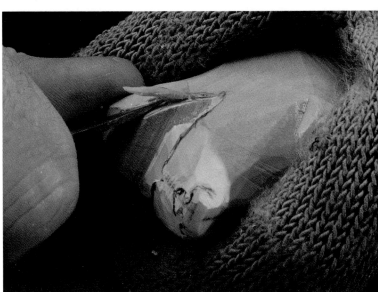

Now make a downward cut to define the lower teeth and lip.

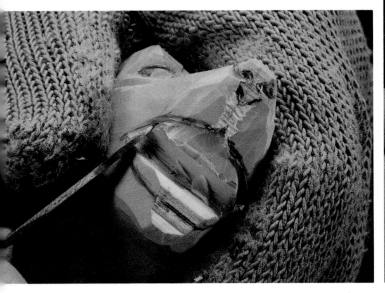

The upper lip should look like this.

Make these cuts all around the lower lip to define it.

Hollow out the roof of the mouth with a small U gouge. When you do this, do not pry against the teeth. Just cut straight in with your chisel.

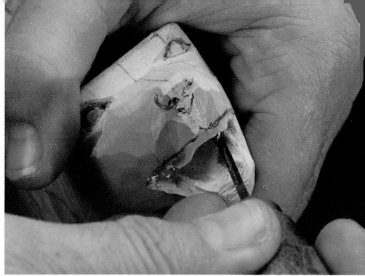

Use the small U gouge to define the inside of the teeth and the edge of the tongue as well. The remaining detail will be provided by the woodburner.

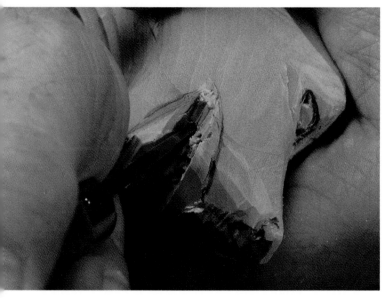

Then turn the small U gouge over to cut into the throat area. The waste material will fall out.

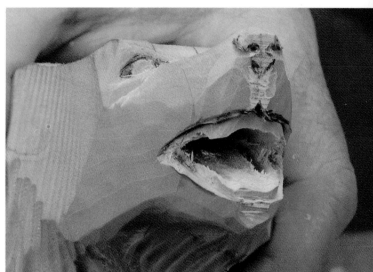

The mouth should look like this at the present stage.

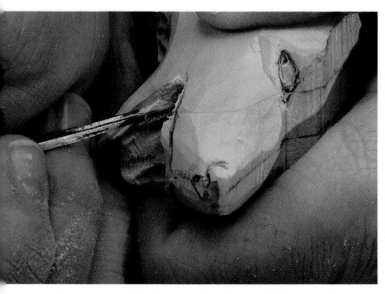

Define the edge of the lower teeth with a small U gouge along the outside of the teeth.

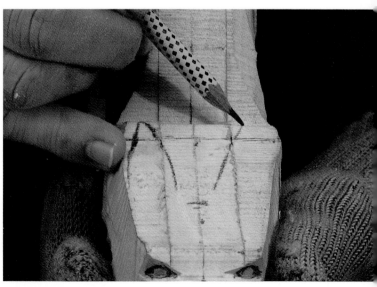

Sketch each ear now by drawing an open V. Draw the ears thicker than they need to be so more waste wood can be removed without damaging or snapping the ears off.

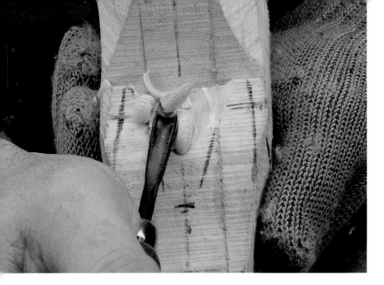

Gouge out the area between the ears with a U gouge from the top of the head to the top of the back.

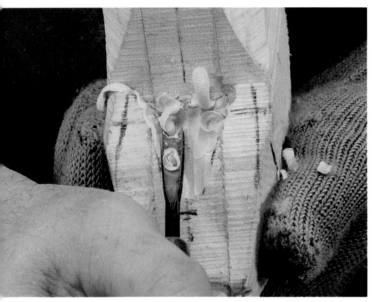

The opened area between the ears should look like this now.

Put in a stop cut along the lower edge of the ears.

Sketch in the side view lower edge of the ears.

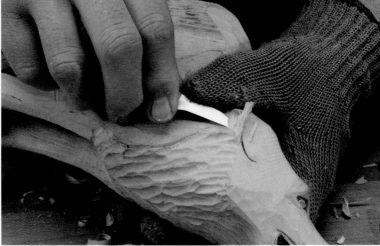

Remove the wood away from the bottom edge of the ear along the stop cut. This will define the ears away from the neck. This also shapes the neck below the ear.

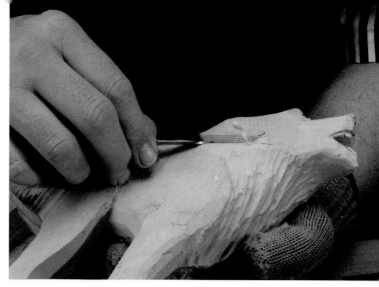

This is how the under edge of your ear should now look.

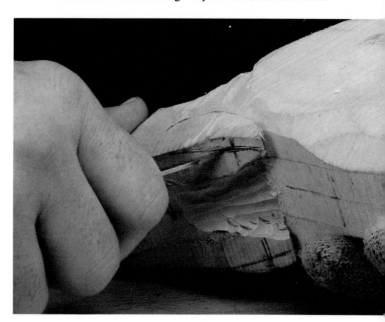

Make a stop cut along the dorsal edge of the ear sketch line.

Continue to clear away beneath the ear.

Now cut back to the stop cut.

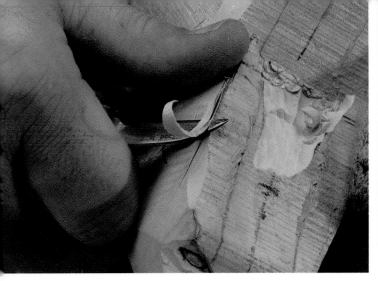

Round off behind the orb of the eye to the front of the ear to define the shape of the skull.

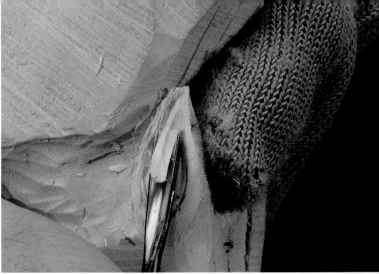

Use a U gouge to hollow out the center of the ear to approximately 1/4 of an inch deep.

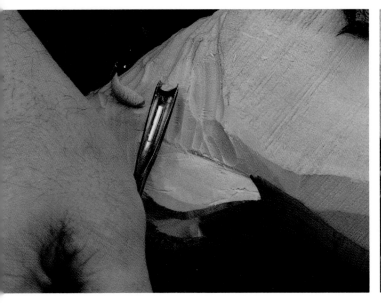

Take a U gouge to extend the ruff up to the ear and define the neck and shoulder area. The U gouge makes a nice round bottomed cut to look like the hair is matted in large clumps.

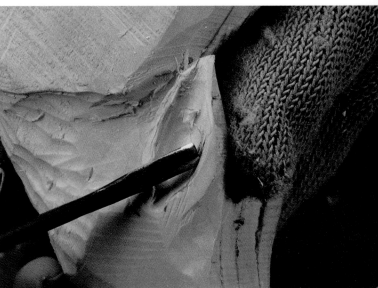

You should end up with a fairly sharp line along the top of the ear and a rounded line along the bottom.

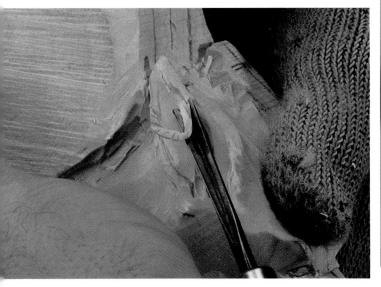

Take a V gouge to form the line along the inner edge of the ear.

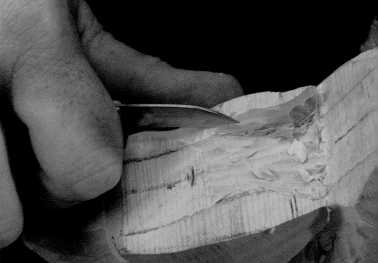

After you have the inside of the ear carved, you can round the back edge of the ear.

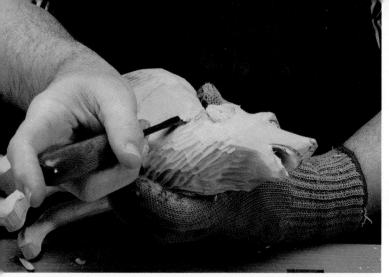

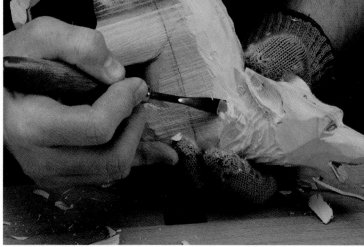

This is how it should look when it is rounded. The sharp top edge should be smoothed down from the center line to the thickest portion at the middle.

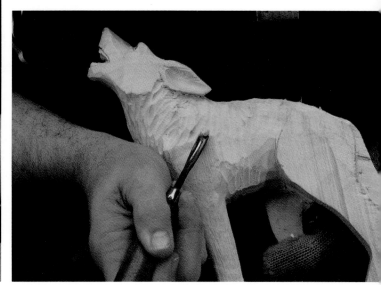

Start rounding off the shoulders with a flat gouge back towards the haunches. Round all the way in to the center line.

Use the U shaped gouge to create masses like matted hair from the center line to the guide line at the thickest portion on the side of the coyote.

You will round down roughly to this point, about half way down the body where you reach the coyote's widest point.

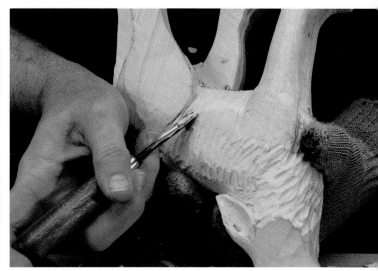

Now work from the guide line down towards the stomach with the U gouge to create more matted hair.

On the front legs, remember to stop shortly past the elbow with the U gouge. From the elbow down the hair becomes more fine and will be put in with the wood burner.

The completed hair should look like this. Remember to align the hair in the direction water would take as it runs across the body.

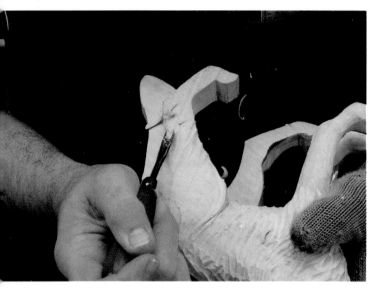

Work down the back legs much farther with the U gouge.

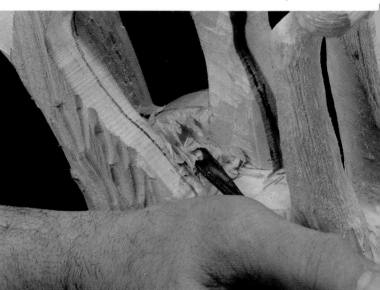

Take a U gouge to clean excess wood from between the back legs in order to be able to reduce the rear legs properly.

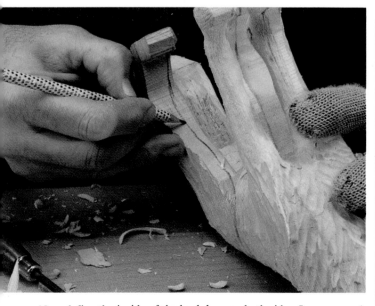

Now define the inside of the back legs on both sides. Leave enough wood to round it, to define the area where waste wood is removed.

Carve a stop cut along the line along the inner edge of the leg.

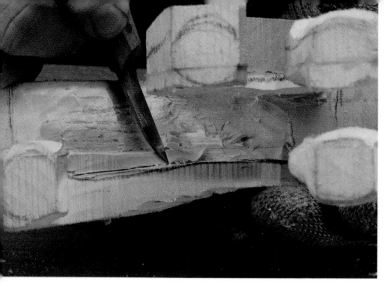

To remove the waste wood along the inside of the rear legs, use the stop cut to guide your blade. Remember to refresh the stop cut as you reduce. Repeat the process on both legs.

Continue to reduce the legs like this. See the thumb supporting the leg so it does not break.

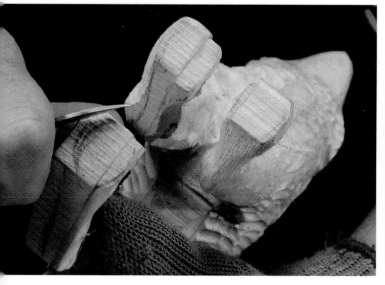

Now round off the back paws.

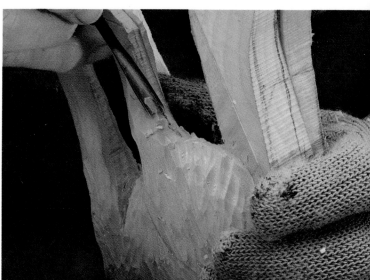

The back leg comes to a point in the rear. The point is the line of the tendon running down the back of the leg. This is defined with a U gouge.

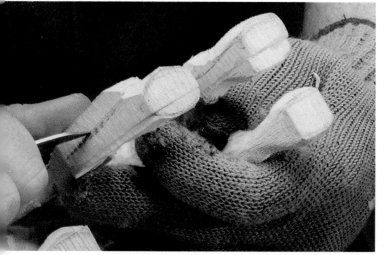

Once the paws are rounded, run a cut line down the outside of the legs and start reducing away the waste wood. Remember to support the leg with your thumb. When you are looking at the back of the rear leg, the joint slopes in towards the center line - making them knock-kneed in reverse.

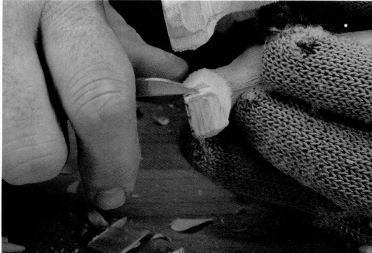

With a bench knife, trim out a small right angle cut to relieve the side of the foot back to start to show the toes.

Sketch the pads on the bottom of all four feet so you will know where to trim back for the toes.

Make a stop cut on both sides of the foot along the sketched toe lines.

Cut a V shaped groove to form the center toes.

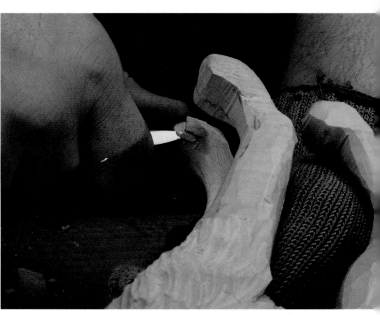

Pare out the toes with just the tip of the knife, working to the cut line. This will define the toes on the outside and inside of the foot. Repeat this process on all four feet.

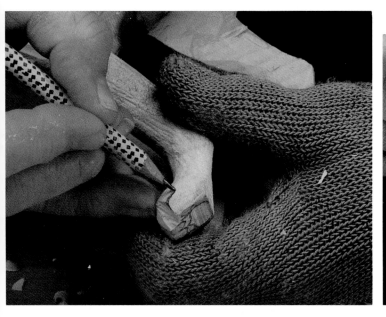

Sketch in the outside toe on both sides of the foot.

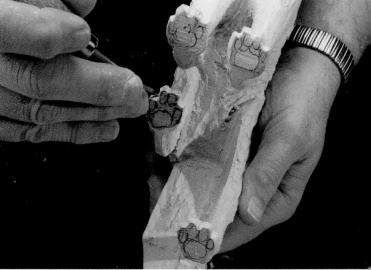

Use a small V gouge to finish all the toes.

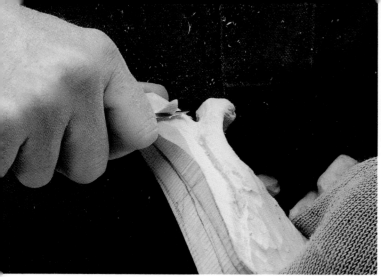

Now, following the guide lines drawn on the tail previously, start rounding the edges off the tail with a bench knife.

Now it is time to add hair masses to the tail. Beginning on the back and working toward the tip with a U gouge, randomly place strokes down the tail to create random hair masses.

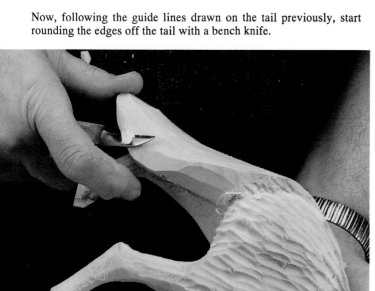

Continue rounding and shaping the tail down. Leave the tail full. Round to the center line of the tail. Make the tail symetrical on either side of the tail. Also be sure to avoid any flat areas on the tail. Make sure it is well rounded.

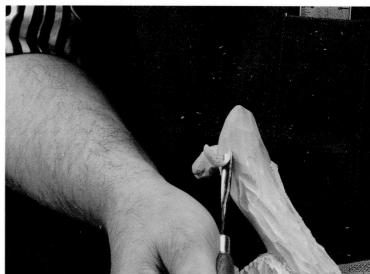

Continue placing tail hair down to the tip.

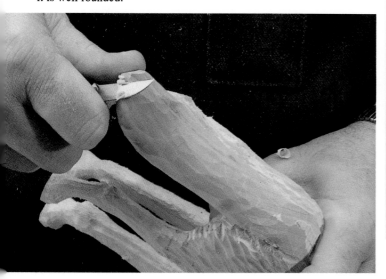

Here is a good view of the rounded tail.

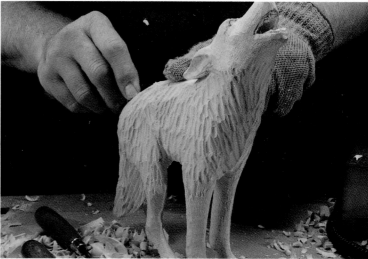

This is how the coyote should look now that the carving is done and before the wood burning begins. For wood burning you need two pens, one heavy for overall burning, the other light for details such as the teeth. The pen shape is your preference.

Burning and Painting the Coyote

Using the wood burner, Square off the lips and darken them to really start to define the mouth.

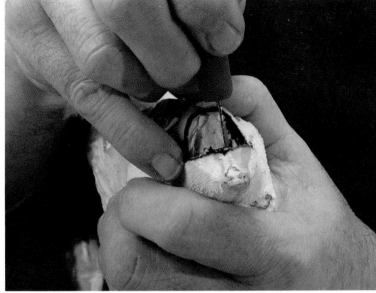

For the front teeth, just burn some little lines between the fangs.

To show the fangs, burn a line on either side of the fang. Any surplus may be undercut and lifted away.

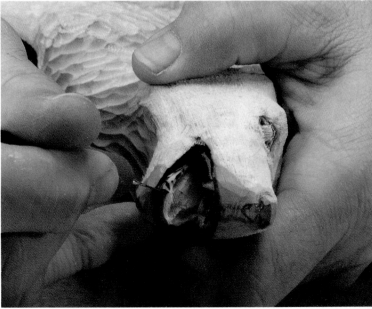

Moving to the lower jaw, burn one cut on either side of the fang to create the lower fangs.

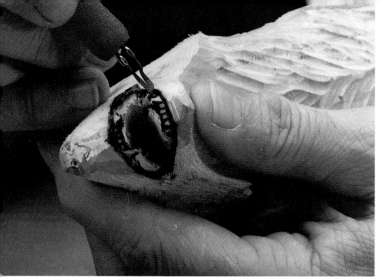

Burn in small, vertical lines to create the teeth.

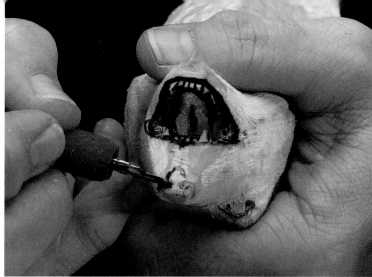

Burn in the nostrils.

Burn a line where the tongue meets the teeth to undercut the tongue and separate it from the teeth on the sides. Also burn in the tongue's center line.

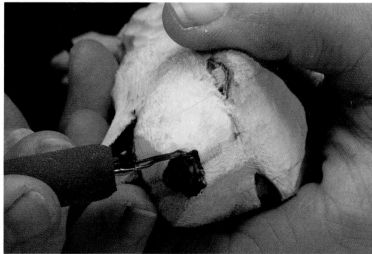

Take the side of the burning tool to color in the nose.

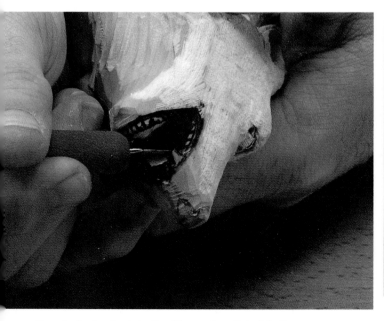

Burn in the top back teeth with a series of straight lines.

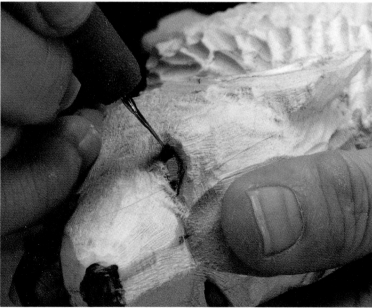

Burn in around the eyes, using the same techniques employed to carve them.

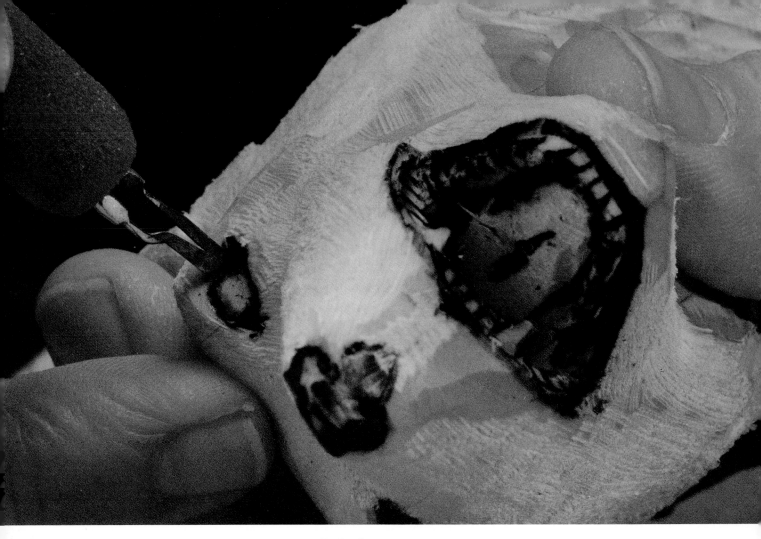

Darken in all around the eyes.

Burn a line along the edge of the inside and outside toes.

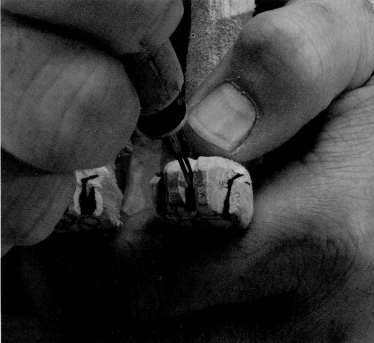

Between the two middle toes you create a cut on the lower sections of the toe with the side of the burning tool. Then at the next joint you do a plunge directly in between the toes. At the next joint up, repeat the plunge. This will make the toes look separated.

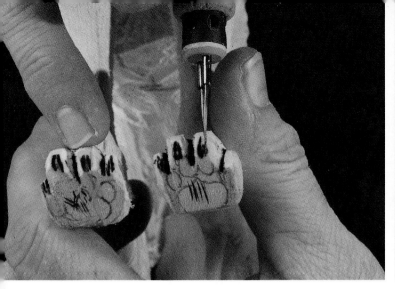

Toe nails are done by making a cut on either side of the center line of each toe with the burning tip.

Now we will burn on the hair on the face. Starting from the nose use very fine strokes, remembering to have the hair follow the contours of the face as water running off the nose would. Try not to line up your strokes. Make them random rather than one long continuous line. Hair doesn't grow that way.

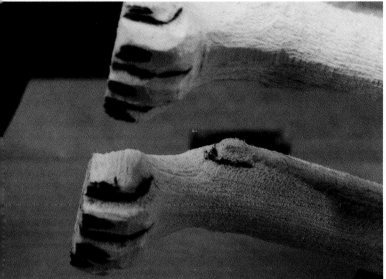

Burn in around edges of the dewclaw as well.

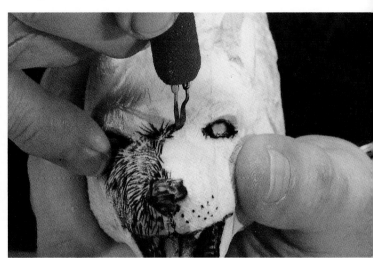

The hair also spirals out from a place between the center of the coyotes eyes; a point of origin just like on the crown found on the human head.

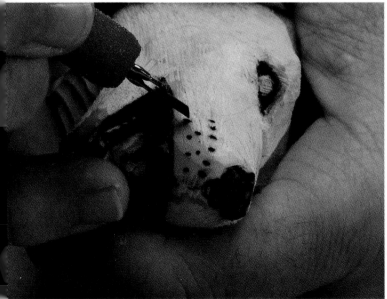

Burn in dots on both sides of the muzzle now to represent whiskers.

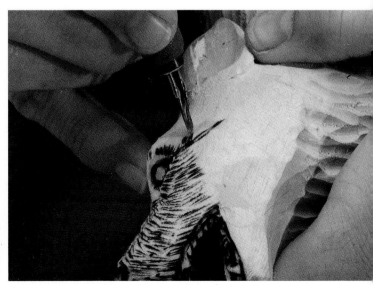

Now burn in the coyote tear line, a line of dark hair coming off the corner of each eye.

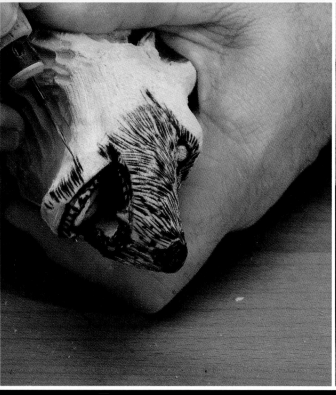

On the underside of the jaw burn in heavier straight hair.

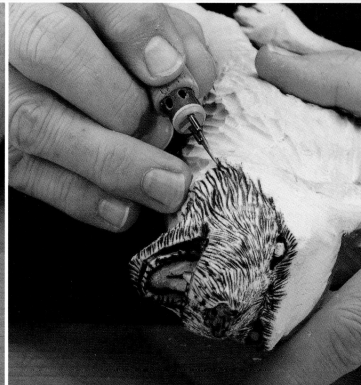

To make the hair look heavier, burn in little Vs. Some of them should overlap and appear wavy.

As you can see, moving down the neck the strands become heavier and larger.

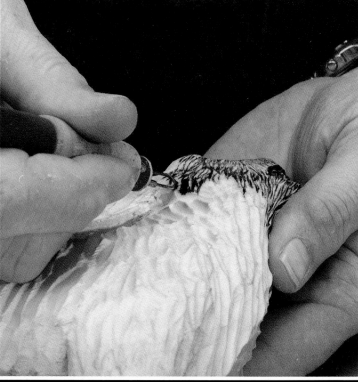

Where you burn down over breaks like the one found at the jawline, burn a cut to produce the effect of the ruff.

Don't despair, you're half way there.

Continue burning matted, heavy hair across the back, over the shoulders and sides, and down on the upper legs.

Continue the random pattern down on the tail, creating a dark tail tip.

On the lower legs the hair becomes fine again as it is on the face.

Here is how the coyote should look when it is burned in.

Painting

To paint the coyote, use acrylic paints and water them down at each step. To cover the entire coyote use raw sienna, burnt umber, yellow ocker, black and white.

To make a base coat to cover the coyote: take raw sienna as the largest amount, add just a touch of yellow ocher, and water it way down. Make it thin enough you can almost read through it. Start at the feet and paint up as a very light wash. Cover the whole animal, keeping the color consistant. This stains the wood without hiding the wood burning. Try to brush the paint in the direction the hair flows. This will prevent collecting any big clumps of paint.

Being careful to get a random pattern on the back, run the hair down off the spine.

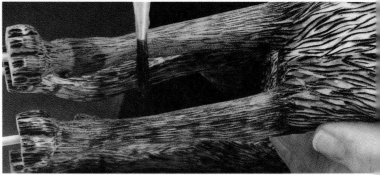

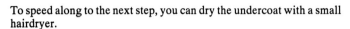

The face has yet to receive the undercoat here. You can see how the body coat looks like a stain and does not hide the burned details.

To speed along to the next step, you can dry the undercoat with a small hairdryer.

Here is how the coyote looks with gray coating the body.

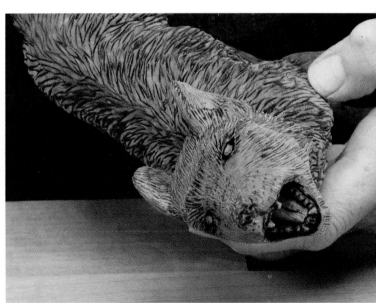

Next, on the legs up to the elbow and on the underside of the tail and on the ears: raw sienna and red. A lot of raw sienna and very little red. Depending on the area of the country, the coloring will change. These are Rocky Mountain colors. From the southwest coyotes are primarily gray with a little yellow. Check with the game department in your area for the color of regional coyotes.

Now mix black and white to form gray, adding a small amount of burnt umber to tint the gray. The burnt umber keeps the gray from being stark. This coats the rest of the body above the legs. Blend in the paint where it meets the leg color to avoid and stark contrast lines.

To a small strip on either side of the nose, and randomly down the middle of the back and over the shoulders, add raw sienna and red. This give the coyote a mottled appearance. The only place this color is very strong is right on his muzzle.

Add a little frosting of white in random splotches throughout. Allow the white to get contaminated with whatever else is on your palate to reduce the stark color.

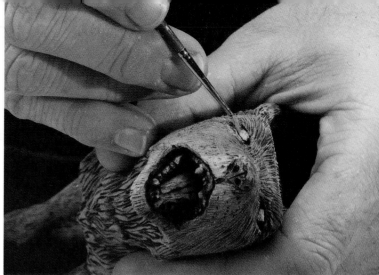

The base coat for the eyes is yellow ocher lightened a very little bit with white.

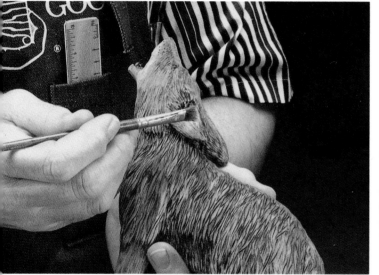

Add a little pure white into the ears and on the upper lip of the muzzle.

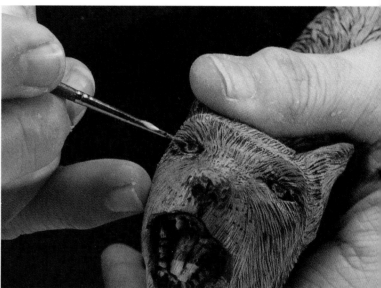

Once the eyes have dried, add a thin raw sienna wash to cut down on the bright yellow color. The pupil is burnt umber.

Now when the paint is dry, dry brush on more white. When you are dry brushing, stroke at 90 degrees to the lines. Put on a very light coat to heighten the highlights and give the illusion of a little glint of light on the fur while tying all the colors together. No definite sharp lines are left.

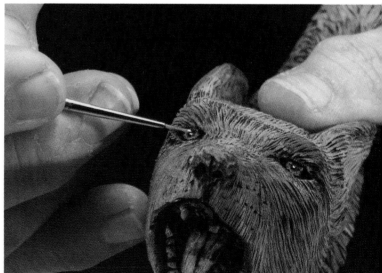

The last color for the eyes is one little spot of white in the pupils themselves.

Paint the nose pure black, do not water it down.

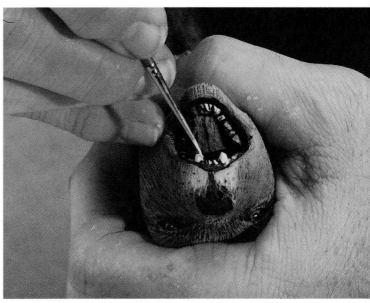

To finish his mouth out paint the teeth, using a very little brush and undiluted white paint. To dilute the white would turn it yellow.

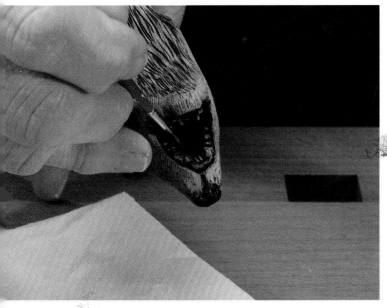

Now paint the roof of the mouth and down the throat dark with an undiluted burnt umber.

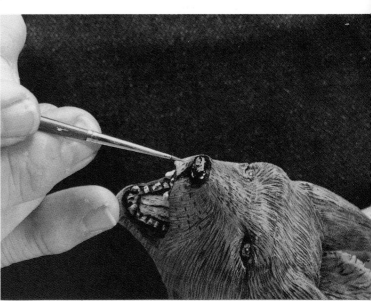

Now put a clear gloss medium on the eyes, nose and tongue to finish the painting. This adds a wet look. Feel free to flood the eyes with the gloss to get the right effect.

His tongue is pink. Dilute the red way down with white to create a very pale pink.

The painting is done.

Now apply clear paste floor wax to liven the coat up and to give the coyote the highlights that bring his coat to life without giving it a hard glossy shine.

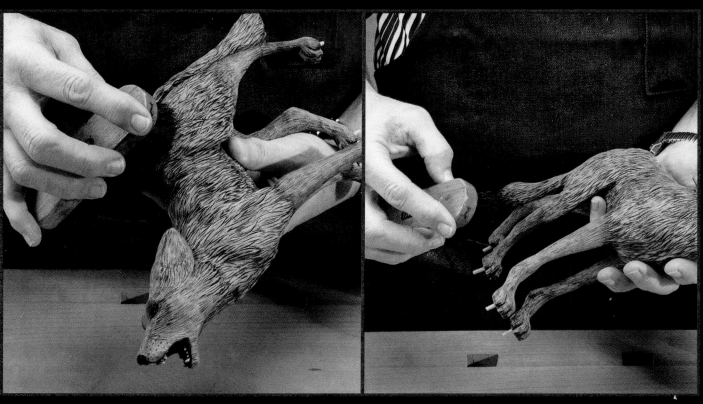

Polish the floor wax with a shoe brush to bring the coyotes coat to life

Your coyote is finished.

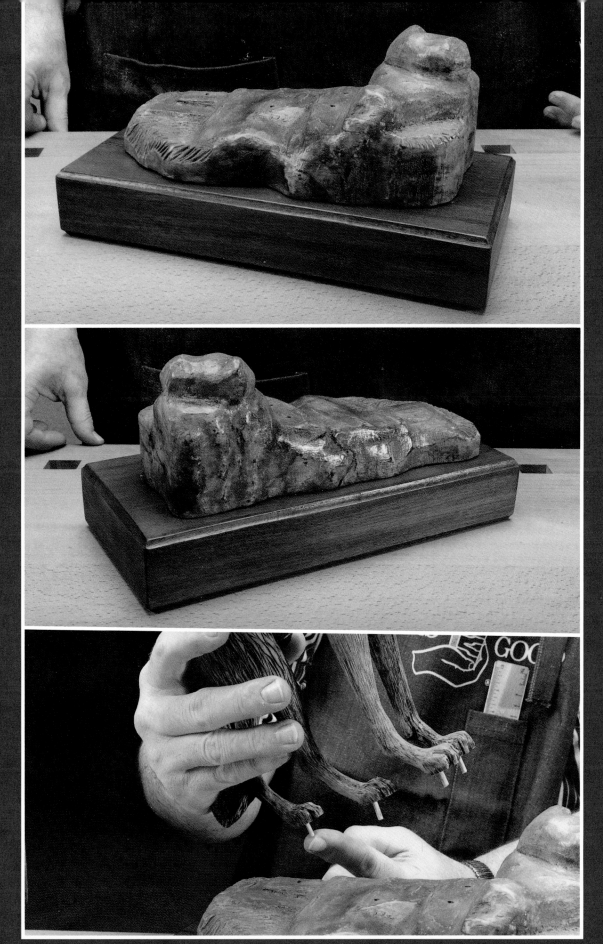

Add 1/8 inch dowling to the bottom of the legs to help secure the coyote to the irregular surface of the base.

The finished coyote.

Carving the Rabbit

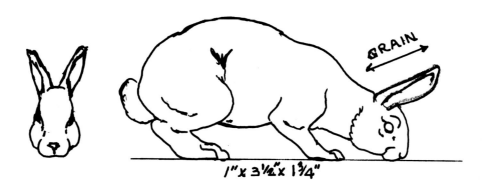

1" x 3½" x 1¾"

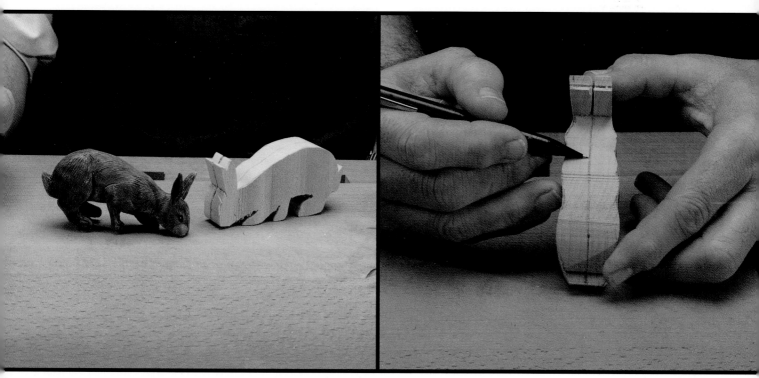

Here is the beginning rough and the finished rabbit to add a little extra interest to your rocky scene.

Make sure your center line is drawn completely around the piece.

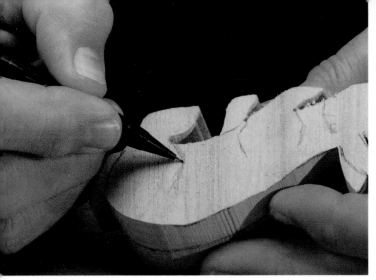

Sketch on the outline of the rabbit.

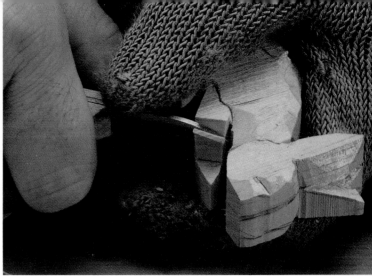

Remove the wood from the side you do not want the foot to appear on.

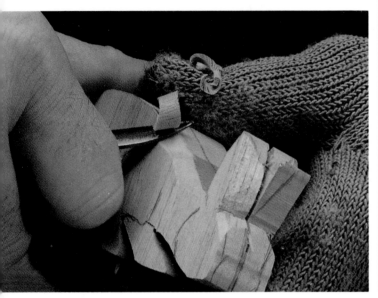

Pick a point and begin rounding off the square corners. But leave the ears for last as they are the most fragile part of the carving.

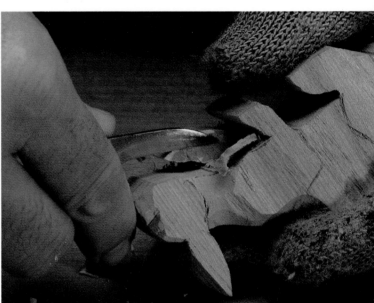

Stop when one half of the wood is removed from the foot.

Scribe in the guide line of the front foot and incise the center line underneath to remove half of the stock from the foot.

Repeat this process with the opposite front leg. This will give you the opposing two front feet.

This is how both front feet should look when you are done wasting away the excess wood. Now draw in the outline of all four feet on their bases.

The rear legs should now be opened up in this style.

Incise a line on the inside of the two rear feet to give you a stop line to work to.

Determine the position of the front shoulder and incise the line along the front shoulder and along the back of the front leg as well.

Remove the wood from between the feet, using your stop lines as a guide.

Clean out behind the back-most front leg to show that it is actually free from the rabbit's body.

Move on down the body, rounding off the square edges up to the center line along the rabbit's back.

Continue rounding the legs now as well, following the foot guides on the base of the feet for size.

Now incise the lines along the rear leg to facilitate rounding off the hind quarters.

Make sure that you leave enough wood to complete the tail. To do this draw guide lines on the back of the tail block.

Round the hind quarters and free the tail.

Remove the excess stock from the tail.

Now that the body is rounded, trim the ears back. You may decide whether they should be both forward, both back or one of each.

Carve out the inner ear with a small U gouge.

A word of caution, do not carve the ears too thin. Round the backs first and then carve the interiors.

This is how the carved inner ear should look.

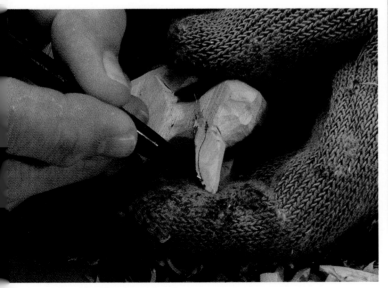

Draw in the shape of the inner ear on the outer surface, which is still flat.

A light sanding with 280 grit sandpaper will smooth the rabbit down to give the carving a finished look. This is how he should look now.

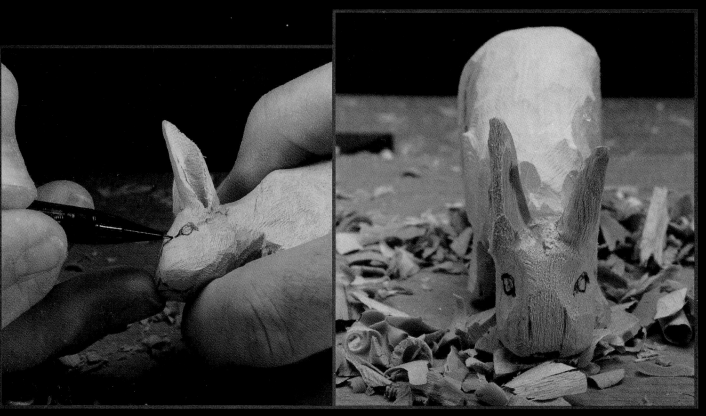

Draw in the eyes below the line of the ear.

Burning the Rabbit

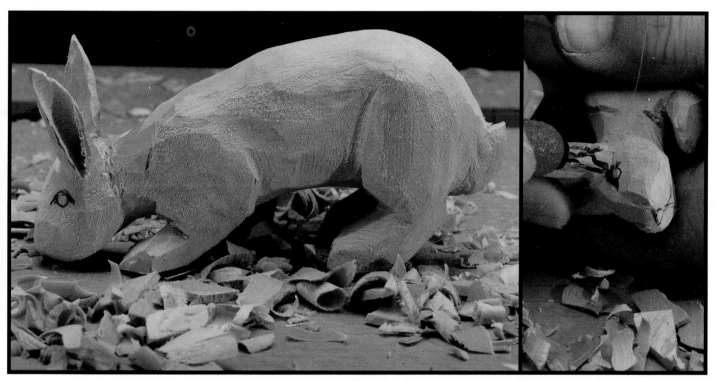

You can either carve the eyes in with a knife (as with the coyote) or you can burn them in.

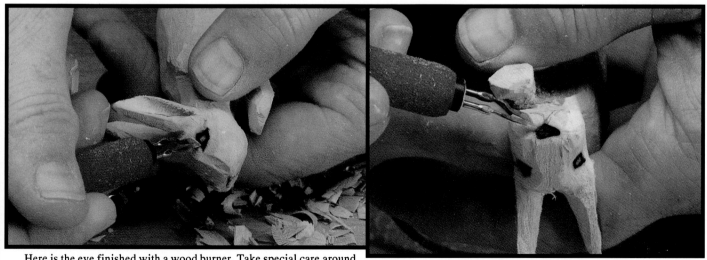

Here is the eye finished with a wood burner. Take special care around the lower eye lid not to burn too much.

The nose is just a small V put in with the wood burner.

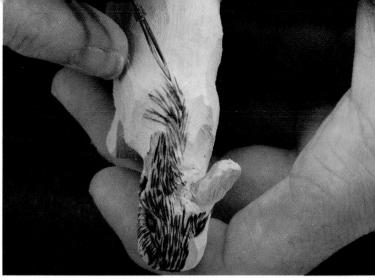

To get the hair in the proper position, think again about how a drop of water would run around the rabbit's body. Remember also to come off the center line along the back. The hair runs from the backbone down.

Burn in the mouth and the whiskers like this.

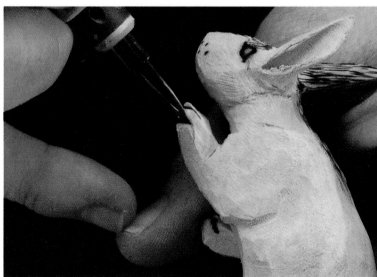

The toes are just like the coyotes toes, there are four. Draw them in and then they may be burned in. They are very straight forward.

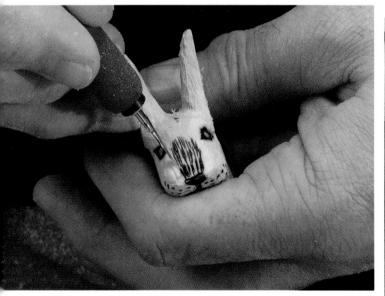

Burning in the hair (if you choose to do so) is just a series of little strokes.

Note the small strokes used to put in the hair.

Here is the rabbit with his fur burned on.

Here are the wood burned and the finished, painted rabbit together. You should paint the rabbit at the same time you paint the coyote. The colors and the process are absolutely the same. The regional coloration for your coyote and rabbit will be the same as well.

The final product.

The Gallery

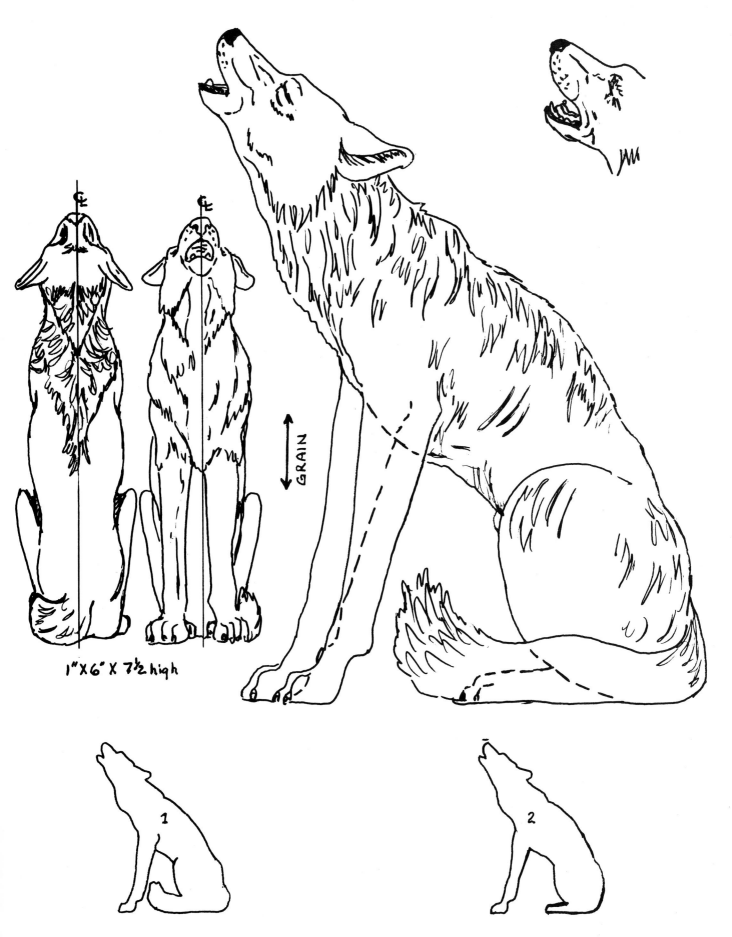

1"X 6" X 7½ high

GRAIN

1

2